LAND OF THE
ICE KING

LAND OF THE ICE KING

CLIVE JOHNSON

CONTENTS

INTRODUCTION
9

CHAPTER ONE
South Atlantic
33

CHAPTER TWO
Shackleton's Island
43

CHAPTER THREE
Into the Ice
93

CHAPTER FOUR
Winter
117

CHAPTER FIVE
The Future
153

BIBLIOGRAPHY
160

First published in the UK in 1990 by Swan Hill Press,
an imprint of Airlife Publishing Ltd.

British Library Cataloguing in Publication Data
Johnson, Clive
    Land of the ice king : an Antarctic journey.
    1.   Antarctic
    I.   Title
    998.0

ISBN 1 85310 143 5

Printed in Singapore by Kyodo Printing Co.
(Singapore) Pte Ltd.

Swan Hill Press

An imprint of Airlife Publishing
101 Longden Road, Shrewsbury SY3 9EB, England.

'Mud, mud, glorious mud!' A young Elephant seal in a mud wallow. This particular pup had to be dug out, as the sides of the hole were too steep for it to climb out, and it would probably have died.

The Antarctic continent is the earth's last almost untouched wilderness. Its harsh climate has so far managed to withstand humanity's endless search for more room and more resources for its growing numbers. Human technology has developed to such an extent that the isolation of Antarctica can now be overcome. But human consciousness has also developed, and Antarctica may well become the cause of the most critical turning point in human destiny. The struggle will be between those who cannot accept that there has to be an end to growth and development and those who have come to understand that this globe of limited size, which we call Earth, is already over-loaded with the present human population and its ever-growing need for more resources.

If the struggle can be won to protect Antarctica, and the seas surrounding the continent from human exploitation, it will mark the beginning of a new and more responsible relationship between humanity and its only home in the vastness of space.

Clive Johnson's brilliant photographs give a vivid impression of the wildness and stark beauty of this great continent. The immediate issue is whether this land is to remain like this, or whether it is to become yet another casualty of the demands of human industry; mine workings, slag heaps, pollution and the seas plundered of fish and wild life. The more important issue is whether humanity will be able to accept that it has finally reached the limit of its expansion.

1990

INTRODUCTION

Antarctica. To most people, the name alone will evoke images of a vast wilderness of ice and snow, a land of great spaces, intense cold and the long polar night — an environment not compatible with human comfort. So why does man seek to further his knowledge of this great white continent, which would appear to be of little or no apparent value to man's continued existence on Earth?

Over the last decade, human activity in Antarctica has increased dramatically and man's presence is now firmly established. No longer is it a remote region, occupied only by small isolated groups of rugged explorers, making long and often very dangerous pioneer sledge journeys, or the preserve of a handful of countries who are wealthy enough to fund research projects in remote polar regions.

Individual reasons for spending long periods of one's life in a harsh, cold and dangerous environment are wide and varied. Some are incited by a keen thirst for scientific knowledge, others simply by a love of adventure and the mysterious fascination of the unknown. Certainly, in my case, it was the latter which attracted me, for who could resist an opportunity to explore the last great, unpolluted wilderness on Earth; a continent of extreme contrasts, whose ice sheet covers more than fourteen million square kilometres and averages more than 3,500 metres in thickness, representing approximately one tenth of the world's total land surface.

Throughout the history of Antarctica, science and exploration have always gone hand in hand. However, as an adventurer I couldn't help feeling a strange sort of guilt that what I was doing was assisting scientists to increase their knowledge of continental geology, which in turn would be of great use to commercial mineral exploration companies worldwide.

In 1909, during one of his fund raising lectures, Captain R. F. Scott was once asked: 'What's the possibility of trade between this town and the Antarctic? Is there anything I can buy or sell?' Now, eighty years later, the answer to that question would have to be 'yes', but to date, due to the regulations and agreements set out in the 1961 Antarctic Treaty, international co-operation and understanding have provided a barrier against the pollution of clumsy commercialism. But for how long?

Since the discovery of the Antarctic ozone hole by the British Antarctic Survey, people have become increasingly aware of environmental problems on a global scale and can see the urgent need to protect and conserve natural environments which are of vital importance in maintaining the life support systems of our planet. The indiscriminate commercial exploitation of Antarctica's delicately balanced ecosystems must now be of great concern to everyone. Antarctica is recognised internationally as a unique natural laboratory, which provides a resource infinitely more valuable to man's future existence than the short term financial gains which would be gleaned by extracting any of the minerals hidden beneath its cloak of ice.

One can only hope that in the next few critical years, common sense will prevail.

Clive Johnson

A 'pod' of Crabeater seals *(Lobodon caracinophagus)*, basking in afternoon sunshine, near to Faraday station which can be seen top right. Using a 28mm wide-angle lens ensured that a good depth of field was obtained and everything in the photograph from just in front of the camera to infinity came into focus.

Opposite: Giant Petrels *(Macronecteus giganteus)* feeding on the remains of a dead elephant seal. Pintado Petrels and Dominican gulls are also waiting their turn to feed off the carcass.

Heavy pack-ice in the northern end of the Neumayer Channel eventually stopped all progress south, and we just had to sit and wait for the wind and sea currents to move the ice.

Overleaf: Beauchêne Island with its vast colony of Rockhopper penguins, *(Eudyptes crestatus)*, locally known as 'Rockies'. The noise from such a large colony is quite deafening. The Rockhopper's call is a short, loud bark and has been likened to the sound made by a rusty wheelbarrow being pushed at high speed! Also nesting with the penguins are Black-browed albatrosses *(Diomedea Melanophris)*, immense seabirds with a wingspan of over two metres. Locally called 'Mollymawks', they feed on squid, Krill and small fish, but have been known to attack wounded or dead birds. With such a large colony of birds goes an equally impressive smell!

Large crevasses on the Nordenskjold Glacier make inland travel hazardous. Bright snow scenes such as this are tricky to shoot and must always be over-exposed slightly to obtain good shadow detail.

Opposite: A towering iceberg held fast in the winter sea-ice of Laubeuf Fjord. It is not unknown for the underside of trapped bergs to become eroded away making the whole berg top heavy, leaving it liable to overturn without warning.

Icebergs and loose pack-ice off the Antarctic coast.

Opposite: Striated Caracaras (*Phalcoboenus australis*),
local name 'Johnny Rooks'. It is a large, dark-coloured
bird of prey and very much an endangered species. The
Falklands may be one of the bird's last breeding
grounds. It feeds on all kinds of carrion, as well as
young penguins and other young birds.

Overleaf: Antarctica is not just a flat, featureless ice-
cap, but a land of spectacular mountainous scenery.
These rock spires are near the British 'Faraday' station
base ('F').

The happy father? Brown Skua gull with a chick and an egg which is just about to hatch.

Opposite: A fully grown bull Elephant seal can weigh up to four tonnes and measure six metres in length. Numbers would appear to be on the increase, after they were slaughtered in their thousands during the nineteenth and early twentieth centuries.

Overleaf: View looking east across Cumberland Bay from the summit of Mount Hope. Some excellent 300 metre snow gullies provide good snow climbs and an opportunity to capture the early morning light from a lofty viewpoint.

Top: A solar parhelia, or 'sun dog', brightens up a hard day's sledging. This solar phenomenon is very photogenic and is common at high latitudes.

Above: The 'Admirals' and 'Players' hauling up the Shambles Glacier *en route* to the now abandoned Adelaide station on the south west coast of the island. Our sledge tracks can be seen leading back to the top of McCallum Pass at top right.

Opposite: Camp on the upper reaches of the Cook Glacier during our main winter manhaul journey to the Ross Pass area. The peak in the background is Nachtigal peak, a satellite peak of Mount Brooker to the left.

Nigel Young drives the 'Huns' into Bourgeois Fjord,
across very solid sea-ice. I kept my camera warm
inside my anorak and was able to snatch two or three
shots at a time before the mechanism started to slow
down and freeze. The temperature on this day was
hovering around −40°C.

Opposite: Our camp on the Fuchs ice piedmont after the
storm. A lot of digging was required to find food
boxes buried under the accumulated snow.

Overleaf: As the hours of sunlight increase, beautiful
wind-sheared clouds catch the light with a bright pink
glow.

The Black-Crowned Night Heron *(Nycticorax n. cyanocephalus)*, known locally as a 'Quawk', is a fairly common bird in the Falklands and is found in many coastal areas, feeding on small fish which it catches in rock pools. It hunts with stealth, patience and dexterity, often managing to catch rats below the sea wall at Port Stanley.

CHAPTER ONE
SOUTH ATLANTIC

The two main islands of East and West Falkland, separated by Falkland Sound, lie about 560 km east of the nearest point in South America which is Cape San Diego on Tierra del Fuego. At latitudes between 51° and 53° South and longitudes 57°30' and 61°30' West, the island's weather is dominated by severe westerly gales, generated from the depressions which blow through Drake Passage into the South Atlantic.

After spending the best part of a month cruising through the Tropics and visiting the sun-soaked coast of South America, Port Stanley comes as a bit of a shock to the system. A permanent chilly breeze makes the air temperature feel much colder than it really is, and even at the height of summer (January) the average temperature only manages to creep up to around 9°C. You may think it sounds a depressingly dull and bleak place, but you would be quite wrong. The Falklands are islands of extreme beauty, wild and windswept, and to me they are strangely reminiscent of the Scottish Highlands. Vast expanses of grassland, with underlying peat deposits to depths of five metres extend inland, while on the coast, large areas of tussock grass border pure white sand beaches, on to which thunders the south Atlantic surf, bringing with it many species of penguin which breed on the island.

During my short stay, I took a walk from Port Stanley out to Mount Tumbledown some four kilometres away. I had been told that the summit rocks would provide some entertaining rock climbing and was not disappointed. For a full day I scrambled and climbed on the summit crags and enjoyed the evening light as the sun set behind Mount Kent, before trudging back to Port Stanley for a few beers in the Globe Bar. It is strange now to think that only a short time later, such a beautiful, tranquil setting was to be the site of a fierce and bloody battle during the final stages of the Falklands War.

To the Falkland islanders, or 'Kelpers' as they call themselves, all land outside Port Stanley, is known as 'The Camp', a word derived from the Spanish word *campo*, meaning 'field'. The Camp is the real Falklands: isolated farms breeding sheep, or 'Stanley Greyhound' as it is locally known. These farms are serviced by boat or the island's air service, and are occasionally visited by the local policeman who patrols his 'Camp Beat' on horseback.

Lying some sixty-four kilometres or so off the south-east corner of East Falkland is Beauchêne Island. As you approach the island, all you can make out are steep cliffs with rocky bays, topped with acres of thick, dark green tussock grass. On closer inspection I found that the whole island was heaving with wildlife, and I could understand why, in 1963, the naturalist Ian Strange thought Beauchêne Island an obvious candidate for conservation and that it should be made a wildlife reserve. Ian Strange campaigned strongly, but it was to be ten years before the island obtained the official protection it deserved.

Opposite: A drinks vendor on Copacabana beach, Rio de Janeiro, Brazil. Rio is a city of divided wealth, where the rich are very rich and the poor are destitute. Brazil is also well advanced in deep sea oil drilling technology and may be the first country to exploit Antarctica's oil reserves.

Early morning city smog pollutes the air over Montevideo. Man made pollution such as this is now finding its way into Antarctica.

On the north side of the island there is an unbelievably huge colony of Rockhopper penguins and Black-browed albatrosses, which stretches along the coast as far as the eye can see. In my photograph, the only thing missing from the penguin colony is the noise and smell! Also breeding on the island are Striated Caracara, or 'Johnny Rooks', to give them their local name. The Johnny Rook is a large, dark-coloured bird of prey, and is an endangered species. The Falklands may be one of the bird's last breeding grounds.

Beauchêne Island was once the home of a large herd of Fur seal, but by the early twentieth century the greed of the sealing industry had totally wiped out the population for their much prized skin. There is also evidence that large herds of Sea Lion once colonised the island, but sadly, they are now in decline, and only a small number of animals live on the island.

Out to the east of Beauchêne Island, 1,400 km across the stormy south Atlantic, is the whale-shaped island of South Georgia. This was to be our next port of call.

Mosaics decorate the side of a building on the lower slopes of Cerro Monte, Montevideo, Uruguay. From now on, we will be heading into much colder conditions to the south.

Opposite: Downtown Port Stanley — very much the outback of the British Empire, with a population that has a strong wish to remain British at any cost. Life in the Falklands is arduous, especially for those involved with farming and I feel that the well-being of the human population should take priority over any commercial or political developments of the future.

Overleaf: A Black-browed albatross chick on its nest pillar, made from mud and grass.

Top: Rockhoppers emerging from grass 'tunnels' in between the vast areas of tussock grass that cover the high ground of Beauchêne Island.

Above: Rockhoppers are extremely good rock climbers and here you can see the marks in the rock made by the beaks and claws of many generations of birds which have climbed this section *en route* to the nest sites.

Opposite: Taking photographs of the Black-browed albatross can be hazardous, as you are at risk of being covered in oily vomit should you come within range.

A solitary bull Sea Lion, one of the few survivors of the huge herds of Sea Lion that once colonised Beauchêne Island, along with large numbers of Fur seal. The commercial sealing industries of the eighteenth and nineteenth centuries disposed of the island's entire Fur seal stocks and all but a small number of Sea Lions.

CHAPTER TWO
SHACKLETON'S ISLAND

'A land doomed by nature to perpetual frigidity.'
Captain James Cook

Looking down into the washbasin at what I had just thrown up confirmed everything our captain had told us about the seas around South Georgia. They were some of the roughest waters in the world and were certainly living up to their reputation — my stomach would vouch for that! Out through the porthole the sea maintained its fury, sleet and seaspray lashing against the glass. To the hardened Antarctic traveller these regions are affectionately known as the 'Banana belt', but at that moment I could think of a few more choice names to call it.

We had just crossed the Antarctic convergence, where one moves from the warmer Sub-antarctic waters into the cold Antarctic zone of the southern ocean. The southern ocean is a broad expanse of turbulent water which surrounds Antarctica, and contains stocks of fish, squid and and krill in greater quantities than those of the rest of the world's oceans combined. The ocean also converts carbon dioxide from the atmosphere into organic matter through the activity of its phytoplankton, making it vital to global processes. Strict regulations on fishing the southern ocean must be implemented if we are to conserve and protect the delicate ecosystems and food chain balance of this valuable resource.

South Georgia is situated in the southern ocean and has a chequered history dating back to 1675, when an Englishman called Antonio De La Roche first sighted the island after being blown off course while attempting to sail round Cape Horn. Almost a hundred years later, international competition was growing in a race to make the first landfall on the 'Great Southern Continent', and to this end the Royal Society had nominated a Scotsman called Alexander Dalrymple to take charge of the British ships which were to make the search. Dalrymple believed that the southern continent was inhabited, and stretched from the temperate regions to the South Pole. Also, he prophesied that the population numbered more than fifty million, all enjoying a warm, lush and fertile climate. The Admiralty, on the other hand, had different ideas about the southern climate and, above all, about who should take charge of the Navy's ships. Not wishing to play second fiddle to a mere sailor, Dalrymple, the scientist, backed out of the project.

Captain James Cook, a Yorkshireman and one time grocer's assistant, was chosen to take command of two ships, the *Resolution* and *Adventure*, which duly set sail from Whitby harbour for the Southern Ocean in 1772. His brief from the Admiralty was short and simple: 'To explore as high a latitude as you please.'

On 13 January 1775, two-and-a-half years later, Cook sighted land. Naturally, at first Cook thought it to be the great southern continent of Terra Australis, but he was to be disappointed. Cook struggled ashore in three locations, one of which is known today as Possession Bay, where Cook took formal possession of the land for the British Crown in the name of King George.

Cook describes the island in his journal as:

> 'An island of no very great extent: a land doomed by nature to perpetual frigidity, a terrain savage and horrible, the wild rocks raising their lofty summits till they were lost in the clouds, the vallies buried in everlasting snow, not a tree nor a shrub to be seen: no not even big enough to make a toothpick.'

Cook's description was no exaggeration, and he was also quick to realise that this small island could never have produced the vast amounts of pack-ice and icebergs that he had seen during the previous years of his voyage. This confirmed to him the existence of land in the far south.

Now, more than two hundred years on from Cook, I was on board a modern, ice-strengthened ship approaching South Georgia and began to wish Dalrymple's prophesy had been correct! But, alas, no such luck — Cook was accurate to the word and South Georgia was the most beautiful example of raw nature that I had ever seen. The inland mountains were wild and virgin, and glaciers swept down from high plateaux to the sea, offering an inviting access road to the island's interior, and not a tree in sight.

Slowly the *John Biscoe* worked her way along the northern coast of the island, until the mouth of Cumberland Bay came into view. As we turned into the shelter of the bay, the sea and my digestive system became much calmer.

A welcoming party of local wildlife came out to greet us: Giant Petrels, known to the whalers as 'Nellies' or 'Stinkers', swooped in on a bucketful of galley waste thrown overboard by the cook; Brown Skua gulls and Cape pigeons hovered over the poop deck offering an open target for my camera. The most impressive aviator without doubt is the Wandering albatross. With a wingspan of around three metres, it is the largest flying seabird. Wanderers breed on South Georgia and all the larger Sub-antarctic islands, returning each year to their natal island to reunite with a breeding partner with which, after several summers of courtship, a life-long pair bond has been formed.

Every now and then a group of Gentoo penguins would appear, 'porpoising' along at great speed, swimming alternately under and over the water, taking in a rapid breath when in the air. It was November and the Gentoo penguins were laying eggs ashore. At this time of year some will already have chicks, each partner taking turns to incubate the eggs, while the other ventures out to sea for food. Having filled its gut with fish, the Gentoo then heads for home, waddling up the beach so full of food that it can hardly walk. On reaching the rookery, the poor Gentoo then has to run the gauntlet through other nesting birds before reaching its own nest, with every other bird having a peck at it on the way. Having eventually located the nest, this worn out, battered specimen suffers the further indignity of having to regurgitate the majority of its catch down the throats of its hungry chicks.

A small wooden cross erected on Hope Point, South Georgia Island, in memory of Sir Ernest Shackleton, who died at Grytviken on 5 January 1922 after suffering a heart attack. His grave is in the small cemetery near to the now abandoned Grytviken whaling station.

I knew that the small team of men who had spent the winter on the island would be awaiting our arrival with mixed feelings. Our ship was bringing fresh supplies of food, fuel and replacement personnel, but most important of all we brought news and letters from home. The arrival of the ship would mark the end of winter and the start of the 'Silly Season', and would disrupt the quiet routine which the base would have developed over the winter, turning their peace and quiet into the organised chaos which a base relief often creates.

With the comforting knowledge that I would soon get my feet on solid ground, I went up to the bridge and observed the scene. As we turned into King Edward Cove, the small line of red and white painted buildings came into view. These buildings were once the administrative offices of the Falkland Islands government, who were in control of whaling operations on the island until they ceased in the mid-1960s. At the back of the cove the now abandoned whaling station of Grytviken could be seen; a tumbledown collection of rusting buildings, which were once the nerve centre of South Georgia's whaling fleets.

English sealers were the first to use Grytviken — or Boiler Cove, as it was known then — and iron boilers called 'try pots' were found there when Captain Anton Larsen, a Norwegian and founder of the Campania Argentina de Pesca (Fishing Company of Argentina), built the first flensing 'plan' or level place at Grytviken, around which the shore factory was erected. This was in 1904, when it was reported that the Grytviken whale catchers rarely had to go out of Cumberland Bay in order to reap a rich haul of whales! However, as the industry neared collapse in the late 1960s it was a very different story, with catchers forced to scour vast areas of ocean on long voyages, with the hope of only collecting a small proportion of their licensed quota.

The decline of the whaling industry resulted mainly from the invention of the harpoon gun by another Norwegian called Svend Foyn. In the form of an evil looking cannon mounted on the bows of the catcher, it discharged a steel harpoon attached to a rope. The harpoon itself was made up of two sections, a long steel shank, with an explosive barbed grenade attached to its tip. When the whale was hit, the two sections would separate and the grenade would explode sending fragments of iron shooting through the whale's body, hopefully breaking its spine and causing instant death. That was the theory but, unfortunately for the whale, gunners were not always that accurate and whales would frequently die slow, agonising deaths. Assuming the whale was killed, it would then be hauled alongside and its stomach inflated with compressed air to keep it afloat while being towed to the shore station for flensing and processing.

The slow annihilation of the southern whales continued, until too few of them were left to support a profitable whaling industry. Now whaling is history in South Georgia and all that is left are the abandoned remains of the shore stations to remind us of the fortunes that were made at the expense of the whale. It was very much a case of making a fast buck, without any realistic thought being given to the future preservation of the species, which would now appear to be in a serious decline, possibly towards extinction.

Soon the bo'sun was throwing heaving lines from the Fo'csle deck, across to the small wooden jetty at the end of King Edward Point. A small group of 'Fids' (a name derived from the initials of Falkland Islands Dependancies Survey, now the British Antarctic Survey) had gathered on the jetty to greet the ship. Solid ground at last!

The next few days were spent resupplying the base. Hundreds of boxes and crates of all shapes and sizes were lifted in cargo nets from deep within the ship's hold and deposited on to the jetty. From here, each box had to be manhandled along a human chain and stacked on to a trailer, to be hauled away by a very old and worn out-looking tractor. The tractor would chug along the track until it reached the appropriate store building, where another human chain would be set into action to unload and store away the supplies. It was a very smooth resupply, only interrupted on one occasion when I was searching in the dark for a light switch and inadvertently activated the base fire alarm!

The main base building, appropriately named Shackleton House, was a three storey construction originally built as administrative offices and a hospital in the late sixties. When the whaling industry ground to a halt, the building was of no further use to the Falkland Islands government, which then handed it over to the British Antarctic Survey, to be converted into a scientific base. In 1968, a party of builders were set to work to carry out the necessary alterations and in November 1969 the first official base commander, Mr Ricky Chinn, arrived to take charge. His various administrative duties, such as customs clearance of all visiting foreign shipping, collecting harbour dues, charging for water taken onboard, as well as being magistrate and official postmaster made him a very busy man indeed! From 1969 to 1982 intense scientific fieldwork was carried out around the island and a peaceful atmosphere prevailed — a far cry from the cruel carnage of the whaling and sealing years prior to 1969 and the inhumanity of war in 1982.

Following the base resupply we were due to sail for Fortuna Bay, to begin the summer fieldwork. We had a couple of hours to spare before departure, which gave me the opportunity to look around the abandoned whaling station at Grytviken. Walking on to the flensing plan my imagination started to run wild. I could see in my mind's eye the huge carcasses being hauled slowly from the water on to the wooden plan and could hear the rattle of the steam winches situated at the rear of the plan. I could imagine that first deep cut into the whales' thick blubber, made by the razor-sharp flensing knives which whalemen were expert at using, and could hear the crackling noise the blubber would make in the frosty air. Looking closely at the wooden plan, I could still see the hobnail marks made by generations of whalers' boots. Now, the flensing plan is home to moss, grass and the occasional penguin or seal.

Many generations of Norwegians, Scotsmen, Englishmen and Argentinians worked at Grytviken, and quite a few died there. They are buried in the small cemetery nearby. In the same cemetery lies the body of Sir Ernest Shackleton, who died at Grytviken on 5 January 1922 after suffering a heart attack. A small wooden cross was erected on Hope Point near Shackleton House by his comrades as a memorial to the great man. The night before his death, Shackleton had arrived at Grytviken in a small sealing vessel called *Quest*, which was said to be ill-suited for an expedition to the south polar ice. At 125 tons, she was said to have been in a poor state: she leaked badly, her engines gave her trouble and it had seemed a miracle that she had reached South Georgia at all. Before he turned in on the night of 4 January 1922 Shackleton wrote in his diary:

'At last, we came to anchor in Grytviken . . . A wonderful evening. In the darkening twilight I saw a lone star hover Gem-like above the bay.'

Overleaf: The vast bulk of Mount Paget dominates the surrounding landscape. At 2,900 metres high it is the highest mountain on South Georgia and was first climbed in 1965 by a British combined services expedition, which also retraced Shackleton's historic trek across the island.

At the Grytivken jetty were three abandoned whale catchers. Two were sunken by winter melt water filling their bilges and bore the names *Albatross* and *Dias*. Tied alongside another jetty was the third, *Petrel*, still afloat and a wonderful example of the large fleets of catchers based at South Georgia which hunted the southern whales to near extinction. Now, *Petrel* is just a curiosity for people like myself to look at and exercise the imagination on.

Walking away from Grytviken, I paused for a while and looked back, trying to work up a mental picture of what the station must have looked like when in full operation: huge plumes of smoke and steam belching from the digesters and steam winches, smoke rising from the whale catcher's smoke stack, but the noise and smell would have been quite unimaginable!

Back on board the *John Biscoe*, geologists were studying maps and packing rucksacks with various bits of equipment, in readiness for our fieldwork at Fortuna Bay. I spent the time it took to steam around the coast to Fortuna Bay down in the hold, sorting out tents, skis, camping equipment, climbing gear and food supplies for our four-week stay ashore.

As we entered Fortuna Bay, Gemini inflatable boats were made ready to transport the field party ashore. From the deck, we searched the shoreline with binoculars to find the most suitable spot to land and set up camp. Finding the right place to camp is not as easy as it may sound. First, you have to find a level spot high enough up the beach to be clear of Elephant seals, and especially the beachmaster bull, who can measure about six metres in length and weigh up to four tons! Careful consideration then has to be made to the camp's proximity to breeding birds, penguin rookeries and so forth. Finally, water should be nearby, preferably the fresh type, as water which has been recently used by an Elephant seal for its daily ablutions makes horrible tea.

Fortunately, it was a calm day and landing on the beach was a simple run in on a long, low swell. This kind of day can fool you into a false sense of security and we camped about twenty metres up the beach on a raised beach platform, well out of any danger from seals or sea — we thought. We were wrong. On one occasion, a storm blew up and waves breaking on the beach sent surges of foaming water up the shingle, crashing against the edge of our campsite, only a couple of metres from the tent.

The 'arch enemy' of the southern whales. Whale catchers such as these hunted the Antarctic whale stocks to near extinction. Now they are just rusting reminders of the mass slaughter carried out by an industry which thought of only one thing — profit.

Another problem arrived in the middle of the night, when around fifty Elephant seal pups, each weighing about a hundred kilograms, decided to occupy our part of the beach, keeping us awake for the rest of the night with their continual snorting, squawking and farting. The next morning was spent evicting every last one of them.

Looking over to the western side of the bay, I could see the rock ridge over which Shackleton and his two campanions Worsley and Crean had travelled on their epic journey to Husvik whaling station, where they hoped to get help to rescue the crew of the *Endurance* which had been crushed by pack-ice in the Weddell Sea. The ship's crew were marooned on Elephant Island 1,200 kilometres to the south of South Georgia and Shackleton, who with five men had sailed to South Georgia in an open boat, then endured a long trek over uncharted mountains to reach Husvik. That was in 1916. Today Husvik is just another abandoned shanty of rusting buildings.

During my stay at Fortuna Bay, I made the trek up to the small col overlooking Husvik and tried to sense the feeling of relief Shackleton and his men must have had when they also stood there all those years ago at the end of their long journey, looking down into the harbour at the tiny buildings which then housed their saviours. Now there are no people nor do the steam whistles sound — all that remains are the buildings, uninhabited and silent.

For the rest of the southern summer, our small group was ferried around the island, from one work site to another, slowly collecting large quantities of rock and fossil samples for later study back in England.

Towards the end of the summer, Dave McDonald and I were landed at a place called Shallop Cove. Dave was a geologist and I his assistant. At Shallop Cove we discovered the remains of an old sealer's 'shallop', or boat. During the sealing days groups of men were landed at beaches where large herds of seal were known to be, and made camp there until all the seal had been shot and rendered down into seal oil. This was done by using large iron boilers or 'try pots' to melt down the seal, sometimes using penguins as fuel for the fire. It is also known that the sealers took live chickens ashore as food, but what they didn't realise was that they were inadvertently transporting ship's mice ashore in the chicken crates.

Mice are now thriving on the Nuñez Peninsula, unable to migrate to other parts of the island because of the Shallop and Esmark glaciers which isolate the peninsula. It was already known that rats occupied the abandoned whaling stations and their surrounding area, as we had caught several at Fortuna Bay which had crossed over the mountains from Stromness, Husvik and Leith Harbour. It appeared that mice were a new discovery.

April marked the end of the summer season on South Georgia and the Royal Research Ship *Bransfield* cruised around the island, systematically picking up all the field parties and returning them to King Edward Point. In true Fid tradition, the end of season party got under way as soon as possible, a truly memorable occasion.

When the ship finally left, twenty-two men were left to winter-over, until the ship returned in about six months. A full research programme kept the base well occupied throughout the winter and for me as a mountaineer/photographer it provided an opportunity to explore the island when its winter covering of deep snow made glacier travel reasonably safe.

The harpoon gun invented by the Norwegian Svend Foyn, with its evil looking barbs and explosive tip. It was an extremely efficient whale-killing tool used by man to hunt the great whales until there were too few left to make it financially worthwhile carrying on.

The base meteorologist was a man called Colin Nichol, whose strong will and deep passion for mountaineering made him an ideal expedition member. Colin and I made several short manhauling journeys out into the mountains, in training for a much longer sledge journey later on in the winter. Hauling a heavy sledge up and down mountains was a soul-destroying pastime, as our store had not been provided with lightweight equipment suitable for manhauling. Most of the gear for sledging was designed to be pulled by dog teams or ski-doos, not by men, and we had to modify most of it to keep the weight down. By August we had perfected our manhauling technique and felt ready to tackle a longer and more serious journey.

September normally provides periods of cold but settled weather, so we planned to manhaul from Sorling Valley to Ross Pass, via the Nordenskjold, Cook, Webb and Ross glaciers which by now had a covering of about two metres of hard packed winter snow and would make good safe sledging 'motorways'. The team was made up of Colin and myself, plus a third member, Grahame Morrison. Grahame was a dour Scotsman and a marine biologist. His quiet manner and steady reliability provided a balance, as Colin and I tended to be strong-minded at times.

We were dropped off at Sorling Valley in mid-September, by the base workboat *Albatross*. The weather was superb and the little boat made the sixteen-kilometre crossing to the south east end of Cumberland Bay in about half an hour. Once ashore, the sledge was packed and we set off for Hound Bay like three carthorses hauling a dray. After only a short distance, the strain of pulling a fully laden sledge had warmed Colin up to such a degree that he was stripped down to his long-johns, and still he was sweating! Six days later we stood at Ross Pass at the junction of the Ross and Brögger glaciers, looking out due west to Annenkov Island and the Hauge reef.

On the return journey, we paid a visit to the King penguin rookery at St Andrew's Bay. It is one of the largest penguin rookeries on the island and a most wonderful sight, with countless birds, both adult and juvenile, huddled together for warmth in their struggle to survive the winter. It was at St Andrew's Bay that Cindy Buxton and her colleague became stranded while making a film, when the island was invaded by Argentina in 1982.

Only a few weeks after our journey to Ross Pass I was standing on the jetty at Grytviken waiting for the *John Biscoe* to come alongside, and I knew that the winter was over and another 'silly season' was about to begin at South Georgia. Through the following summer I worked as a field assistant with a geomorphologist called Gordon Thom, another Scot who came from Peterhead. During our summer programme we repeated the return journey from the Ross glacier to Sorling Valley, but in summer conditions it was a totally different journey. Open crevasses and deep soggy snow made the travelling very dangerous indeed. On one occasion, we both found ourselves standing on a crevasse bridge which slowly started to sink and collapse!

The 'flensing plan' at Grytviken. It was on this level area that whales were cut up or 'flensed', prior to being processed in the cookers that are situated at the rear of the plan. Huge steam driven winches can be seen at the back of the plan, which were used to haul the giant 100-ton Blue, Fin and Sie whale carcasses up on to the plan for flensing. All this has now stopped, but it would appear to be too late for the continued survival of the great whales.

South Georgia is certainly an island of extremes; cold and fiercely Antarctic in winter, with violent catabatic winds and heavy snowfall, which make the South Georgia mountains extremely dangerous due to severe avalanche danger. However, in summer the island is transformed into a wildlife paradise. Coastal areas become lush and green, Elephant seals fill the beaches and birds begin to breed. The nineteenth-century sealer Robert Fildes summed up the islands of the southern oceans when he wrote: 'When She fashion'd this place, methinks Madame Nature had been drinking too much!' Fildes was only describing the Sub-antarctic islands, so I wonder what he would have written had he seen the Antarctic continent itself.

A sealer's 'try pot', at Grytviken.

Opposite: The Royal Research Ship *Bransfield* in King Edward Cove, a natural harbour and the perfect site for shore-based whaling operations. British sealers were the first to use Grytviken, or Boiler Cove as it was known then, and iron boilers (try pots) were found there when the first whaling operations began in 1904.

Above: A King penguin (*Aptenodytes Patagonicus*), distinctive with its bright orange comma-shaped ear patches, golden breast feathers and silver grey back. A fully grown adult would measure about eighty centimetres in height and weigh around twenty kilograms. Kings breed throughout the Sub-antarctic islands and were once killed in their thousands for their oil. Sealing vessels would visit colonies in Spring and Autumn, set up 'try pots' and corrals into which the birds would be driven before being clubbed to death. One King penguin produced about a pint of oil, and at that time (around the 1850s) one gallon of oil would bring two shillings and sixpence. It is known that one vessel could annually destroy around 70,000 birds.

Kings have the problem of trying to raise a large, slow-growing chick in an environment where, for half the year, food is scarce. They solve the problem by laying their large single egg in November, with the male bird taking charge of the first incubation period, holding the egg on top of its feet covered with a thick fold of skin. The parents then alternate every four or five days, until the chick hatches, normally in about fifty-five days. The new-born chicks grow steadily and become covered in thick brown wool. By May the parents leave and all the large chicks huddle together in créches for warmth, visited by one or other of the parents about every second or third week throughout the winter. The larger chicks survive the winter well, but there is a steady mortality rate among the smaller birds. By December the surviving chicks are in full moult and leave the colony independent of their parents.

Right: Growing chicks instinctively try to hide under the parents skin fold.

Opposite: An adult King penguin, showing the fold of skin covering an incubating egg.

Gentoo penguins *(Pygoscelis papua)* on South Georgia
Island. The adult has just returned to the nest after a
feeding trip at sea. The chicks perform a beak tapping
ritual as a signal that they require feeding and the adult
then regurgitates food which the chick takes from its
crop. Gentoos are very inquisitive and will often waddle
right up to you if you remain still, but when you move
they will panic and run away. Their nests are usually
among tussock grass and often quite a long way inland.

Opposite: Gentoo penguin 'sky pointing' in an ecstatic
display while making a loud trumpeting call. Within the
colony the adults seem to take it in turn to display.

The Chinstrap or Ringed penguin *(Pygoscelis antarctica)*, sometimes called a 'bearded penguin'. Chinstraps are plentiful on the islands of the Scotia arc, but only breed in small numbers on South Georgia.

Opposite: A bull Elephant seal *(Mirounga Leonia)* in a typical threatening posture, with fully inflated proboscis. Air is expelled through the proboscis and is made to resonate in the sound chamber formed by its gaping mouth. This produces an extremely loud roaring sound.

Top: A Giant Petrel chick in moult. Known to the whalers as 'Nellies' or 'Stinkers', they are true scavengers, eating all kinds of carrion, such as dead seals and penguins, ships' refuse, squid and crustaceans at sea. They have also been known to kill young penguins and to take penguin eggs. They suffer from gluttony and often eat so much that they can hardly stand up, having to regurgitate considerable quantities of food before they are able to walk, let alone fly!

Above: The remains of an Elephant seal after the scavenging birds have finished with it. Eventually the bones will be washed out into the sea.

Opposite: An adult Southern Fur seal. These are now well established on South Georgia, after being almost wiped out by the seal hunters of the eighteenth and nineteenth centuries for their much prized fur. This recovery is good news because on other islands, such as Beauchêne Island, the Fur seal never recovered.

A young Southern Fur seal among the tussock grass of South Georgia. They look quite tame and playful, but can run fast through tussock grass and possess very sharp teeth!

Opposite: The South Georgia Pintail, a close relative of the Brown Pintail of South America. It is common in all the coastal tussock flats of South Georgia and feeds on insects, worms and plant life.

A pair of Brown Skua gulls *(stercorarius skua)*, strongly territorial birds seen here in full aggressive display. If you approach a skua nest the adult will fly away and then start to dive-bomb you at great speed, squawking continuously, until it has seen you off.

Opposite: The Light-mantled Sooty albatross *(phoebetria palpebrata)* is a beautiful-looking bird, with a distinctive white crescent-shaped mark around its eye. They are a common sight on South Georgia, feeding on squid and fish.

The fine art of camouflage is skilfully displayed by this young Antarctic tern. Terns nest in gravel and on glacial moraine, where the young fledglings match the background precisely, making them difficult to find.

Opposite: Two immature Blue-eyed cormorants (*Phalacrocorax articeps*), one of two species of cormorant breeding in Antarctica.

The jaw bone and vertebrae of a whale litter the beach in Moraine Fjord, South Georgia, near to the snout of the Harker Glacier with its thirty-metre high ice pinnacles. Taking photographs on days like this is pure pleasure.

Opposite: The Reindeer is not a native of South Georgia, but was introduced by Norwegian whalers to be used as a fresh meat supplement to their diet. They now thrive on the coastal lowlands, close to the abandoned whaling stations.

Overleaf: A panorama of Mount Paget.

Royal Bay was the base site of a German expedition organised by the German scientist Neuymayer in 1882, from which the party observed a transit of Venus. The remains of the base hut can be seen in the foreground.

Opposite: A fiery sky at sunset on the south coast of the island. For shots like this, the exposure must always be bracketed, as you may never get another chance!

Strong Sub-antarctic winds whip plumes of snow from
the summit and high ridges of Mount Cunningham,
named after John Cunningham who was a member of
the original South Georgia survey expeditions, led by
Duncan Carse.

Opposite: Early morning on the Nordenskjold Glacier
during a winter manhaul sledging journey. We were
glad to be moving after a sleepless night with winds
battering the tent at over 100 knots. This was a training
journey in preparation for a much longer expedition
later on.

Overleaf: Glaciers pour down from the island's
mountains and plateaux, ending in high ice cliffs at the
water's edge, effectively isolating peninsulas of land
and stopping the migration of Reindeer, mice and rats
to other regions of the coast.

Top: Working our way through the seracs of the Harker
Glacier, during the first ever crossing in 1976.

Above: Manhauling off the eastern edge of the
Nordenskjold Glacier in bad weather at the end of our
return journey from Ross Pass. Always carrying a small
compact 35mm camera in my anorak pocket made
taking a shot like this quick and simple, when taking
photographs is probably the last thing on your mind.

Opposite: Looking across Moraine Fjord to the Harker
and Hamberg glaciers, with Mount Sugartop in the far
distance rising to 2,500 metres. This is what mountain
travel is all about.

Looking across Cumberland East Bay to the southern
half of the Allardyce range. From left to right: Mt
Brooker, Mt Kling, Nordenskjold peak and Mt Roots.
These are important mountaineering objectives of the
future.

Opposite: The ice-fall of the Harker Glacier, looking up
to the unclimbed Hendriksens buttress.

Cheap accommodation! The old post hut was once used as a drop-off point for mail being collected at intervals by the men from Ocean Harbour whaling station situated on the opposite (east) side of the Barff Peninsula, some five kilometres away.

Opposite: A bull Elephant seal at Sorling Valley. To give you an indication of its size, the man in the picture is almost two metres high.

Sunset over Cumberland West Bay from the top of
Hodges Glacier. It's worth a sweaty climb and a long
cold wait if you want to be in the right place at the right
time for spectacular photography.

Opposite: Sunrise over the Barff Peninsula, with a
Gentoo penguin colony in the foreground. It was a very
cold morning and a long walk, but the result was worth
it.

The huge King penguin colony of St Andrews Bay in September. The adults are now separated from the chicks and feed them only every second or third week. Some of the adults wander high on to the glacier. The chicks, covered in their thick brown woolly coats, huddle together in crèches for warmth and will soon start to moult with the onset of spring.

Opposite: Much serious scientific fieldwork is carried out throughout the winter on the local glaciers. Here a glaciologist is drilling holes into the glacier ice into which aluminium poles will be inserted. The position of each pole is then accurately surveyed at measured intervals to calculate the movement of the glacier. It is cold, laborious work, often in very isolated locations.

A solar halo, produced by sunlight refracting through
ice crystals in the atmosphere.

CHAPTER THREE

INTO THE ICE

'Out of whose womb came the ice?
and the hoary frost of heaven, who hath gendered it?
The waters are hid as with a stone,
and the face of the deep is frozen.'

Job 38, 29.

Heading south west from South Georgia, towards the northern tip of the Antarctic peninsula through the southern ocean and eastern edge of Drake's passage, was one continuous battle against strong prevailing westerly gales, and powerful surface currents. Each day grew a little colder than the last, rain turning to freezing sleet and then to snow. Thick, dark, grey clouds and turbulent, foaming seas provided a depressing seascape. Below deck, anything not tied down slid about — cups fell from tables, and pots and pans rattled about in the galley cupboards. At times the ship went almost bows under, sending violent pulsating vibrations through the hull, as it ploughed its course south through mountainous waves.

I ventured out on deck whenever possible, which wasn't very often, and was amazed at the variety of sea birds which followed the ship this far south. Great Wandering albatrosses glided effortlessly between the waves, occasionally clipping the surface of the water with one wing before disappearing into the mist. Cape pigeons, Antarctic Fulmars, Prions and Storm Petrels followed the ship for mile after mile, flying low over the crest of the waves.

Icebergs are an ever-present danger to all shipping in the Southern ocean. Tabular bergs, with sides over twenty metres high and very often several kilometres long, 'calve' off the vast ice-shelves which cling to the coast of Antarctica and drift slowly north. At night, tabular icebergs can easily be spotted by the use of radar, but it is the large chunks of ice known as 'growlers' which are too small for radar to detect that cause problems. All night long, a large powerful searchlight attached to the foremast scanned the water ahead, picking out larger growlers in time for the ship to take avoiding action. Up on the bridge, the only sound was the high-pitched whine of the radar scanner, and the tic, tic, tic of the repeater compass which stood directly in front of the ship's wheel.

On the evening of the third day, there was a sudden 'clang', a sound rather like a large steel door slamming shut, followed by a sinister scraping noise alongside the hull. I ran up on deck and in the evening gloom could see the ghostly white forms of ice-floes slowly drifting by. We had reached the pack-ice belt, which was poetically recorded by Ernest Shackleton:

'The crash of the bows in the pack-ice;
The sob of the tilted floe;
The creak of the weighted sledges;
The whine of the dogs as we go.'

Pack-ice surrounds Antarctica in a fringe hundreds of miles wide, forming a major obstacle to shipping early in the season. It is produced during the austral winter, when on calm days the intense cold freezes the surface water in countless fjords, inlets and bays around the coast and out in the open sea itself. Snow falling on to this young 'frazil-ice' does not melt. This is due to the temperature of sea-ice being around −1.9°C, which has the effect of refrigerating any snow which accumulates on top of it. However, the sea is never calm for long and sea swell splits the new ice into small 'pans', whose edges become crumpled and turned upwards as they bump into each other. This is known as 'pancake-ice', which is the youngest form of pack-ice. Pancake-ice is not a serious problem to a modern ice-strengthened ship, which will easily slice through it, making only a faint whispering sound, to leave a long, clear track of open water astern. However, when the sea becomes calm once more, the young pancakes freeze together in clusters, collecting even more snowfall which consolidates them, forming thick, solid floes, and transforming the fragile pancake-ice into hard pack-ice.

Pack-ice guards the approaches to Antarctica for most of the year. A clue to the presence of pack-ice beyond the horizon is given to the mariner by a phenomenon known as 'iceblink'. This shows as a white glow on the horizon, caused by light reflecting off the distant pack-ice.

At first light the following day we were in sight of Smith Island, glowing pink in the early morning sunlight. Large areas of loose pack-ice stretched to the horizon, making any areas of open water as calm as a mill pond. What an amazing contrast, to be transported from the dull, depressing, almost frightening turbulence of the southern ocean, into the full beauty of a polar landscape. Now there was a powerful whiteness all around, broken only by open leads of ultramarine water.

Down below there was an air of excitement, as people unpacked their polar boots and anoraks in preparation for a chilly day on deck sightseeing. For a full day we sailed down the Gerlache Strait towards the Neumayer Channel, which gave everyone the opportunity to soak up the grandeur of the Antarctic, which was to be our home for the next year-and-a-half. We sailed through deep, narrow channels, fringed with ice cliffs over a hundred feet high. The coastal mountains rose to around 2,000 metres, with glaciers sweeping down their valleys from high plateaux, forming a torrent of huge seracs, hanging glaciers and ice-falls. When caught by sunlight, the ice glistened with every shade of green and blue, but in shadow it was jet black. From time to time there would be a loud roar as one of the surrounding ice-cliffs 'calved' into the sea, sending a semi-circular wave rolling out into the channel.

After a final push through some very heavy pack in the Neumayer Channel, which resulted in a bent propeller blade, we anchored off Port Lockroy at 60°49′ South. The abandoned base buildings of Port Lockroy (base A), stand on small, low-lying islands in the bay. Built in 1944 during 'Operation Tabarin', it was the first British Antarctic base and was occupied almost continuously until its closure in January 1962.

For two days, equipment and stores were ferried ashore. New ski-doos were unpacked from their crates and assembled, ready to be flown south to Adelaide Island as a 'tin dog' replacement for the outmoded, but much loved, dog teams. Once all the cargo had been taken ashore, the *John Biscoe* sailed north to make repairs to her propeller, leaving our small group occupying the field hut at Damoy Point. Our job for the next few days was to ferry stores and equipment from the shore up to the airstrip on the ridge of the island and load it on to aircraft, which would then transport it south to Rothera Base on Adelaide Island. Soon, it would be my turn to fly south.

Climbing on top of packing cases in the tail end of a Twin Otter to find somewhere comfortable to sit was not my idea of modern air travel. I was deafened by the roar of engines as the pilot jockeyed the plane into take-off position at the southern end of Damoy Point, almost on to the lower slopes of the island's mountains, pausing only to make pre-flight checks to the engines and flight controls prior to take-off.

This was to be my first experience of flight, and it looked as if it would be a true baptism of fire! Gazing out of the window I could see the ice-cap dropping steeply away on both sides down to the sea. A short, narrow snow ridge ending in a vertical drop of ice cliffs was to be our runway.

I secretly prayed that some sort of fault would be found and the flight aborted, but as I prayed, the pilot's hand reached up to the throttles and pushed them forward. The noise was unbelievable and spindrift totally obliterated the view from the windows as the engines revved up to full power. The aircraft moved sluggishly at first under its heavy load, but picked up more and more speed as it bounced along the airy runway, the ski-equipped undercarriage rattling and banging over the uneven surface. Suddenly the undercarriage noise faded and the pilot eased back the throttles. We were airborne.

Looking out of the window, I saw the ice cliffs at the end of the runway pass underneath. A group of Crabeater seals basking on the pack-ice beneath the cliffs, seemed unimpressed by the annual return of this very noisy species of bird. As the tiny aircraft slowly gained altitude, more and more of the spectacular Antarctic landscape came into view.

Before leaving England, I had attended lectures on Antarctic topics and had spoken to many people who had recently returned from extended tours there. I had also read just about everything I could lay my hands on which related to Antarctica, with the hope of giving myself an idea of the dramatic grandeur I was told I would experience. That afternoon, as we flew down the west coast of the Antarctic peninsula, I felt very insignificant indeed against the size and power of such a vast, raw wilderness. Images of the early explorers such as Charcot in his ship the *Pourquoi Pas* and John Rymill in the *Penola*, who mapped this coastline, came to mind.

From my lofty viewpoint, the majestic beauty was beyond my wildest imagination. Torrents of ice cascaded down from the mountains and from the polar plateau itself, ending in tottering seracs and ice-cliffs which resembled rows of pure white skyscrapers sliding silently towards the sea.

When my ears started to pop, I knew we were beginning the long descent on to the ski-way on Adelaide Island. The landing area was situated some six kilometres from Rothera Base, on an ice plateau above the Wormold ice piedmont and at an altitude of around 275 metres above sea level. With such a large area of smooth snow to land on, touching down was a pleasant experience. After taxying to the parking area, we were met by a group of men, some of whom had spent the last two years living and working at Rothera, and it was interesting to note just how well they had acclimatised to the cold polar climate — at the airstrip the air temperature was hovering around −20°C and they were quite happily working in their shirt sleeves. As an unacclimatised newcomer I felt the need to wear most of my clothing issue!

I hitched a lift on the back of a ski-doo, which followed a flag-marked route below a low, rocky ridge to the top of a long, steep ice ramp, which led down to Rothera Base. Here we stopped and I took photographs of the base while listening to the eerie howl of the forty-seven sledge dogs which still remain at Rothera.

Dogs, as a form of transport were used extensively by British survey teams until 1974, when they were replaced as field transport by motorised ski-doos. The reasons for change were quite simple: a ski-doo is much faster than a dog team, you don't have to feed it when it is not working, and after only a very short period of instruction anyone can drive one. However, to a romantic like me the challenge of driving a dog team in Antarctica was irresistible.

The present stock of dogs are relatives of the first twenty-four animals introduced to Antarctica during 'Operation Tabarin' in the mid-1940s. Some people would argue that there is still a valuable place for dogs in Antarctic exploration and I would agree that in certain situations dogs are a much safer form of transport than ski-doos. But in the short Antarctic summer, speed is essential to complete the increasing volume of scientific programmes which are scheduled each year. Sadly, the running of dog teams is now only a form of recreation, used by base members on their days off.

Rothera Base, named after John M. Rothera, who surveyed the area

Heading south into the Antarctic Ocean, a region of cold, turbulent waters surrounding the Antarctic continent. Ploughing headlong, day after day, into strong westerly gales was quite frightening for a non-sailor like me, but at the same time strangely exciting. The decks are continuously awash, and below deck everything that is not tied down falls about.

between 1956 and 1959, was first used in 1975, when a small base hut was erected and occupied by four men until the main building could be shipped down the following year. Bit by bit, the base has grown in size to become Britain's largest Antarctic station and the centre for all field operations in the British Antarctic Territories.

Modern stations are a far cry from the spartan accommodation of early polar explorers. Rothera is a sort of 'upside-down' building; you live and eat upstairs and the sleeping accommodation is downstairs. No hardship is attached to living there; the buildings are tripled glazed and centrally heated. The base boasts a bar, showers, a comprehensive library, drying room, surgery and even a darkroom — a man-made oasis in a wild and harsh, yet strangely friendly, landscape.

Once I had arrived on base, there was a short period of familiarisation. Instruction in ski-doo driving techniques and first line maintenance was given by the base mechanic, then two 'field-prepared' machines were handed over to me, with a threat of extreme personal violence should I fail to return them at the end of the season in good running order! All

other equipment required for a season's fieldwork had been very carefully prepared by the wintering field assistants and included pyramid tents, dehydrated food, cooking equipment, climbing and crevasse rescue gear, sleeping bags, crevasse probes and a mountain of other 'clatch', which for some reason beyond my comprehension was deemed essential to sustain life for the duration of an Antarctic field season.

Food rations, clothing and tents don't seem to have changed much in design since Captain Scott's day. Woollen underclothing covered with a windproof cotton anorak and overtrousers still appears to be the most practical combination to cope with the cold, dry Antarctic climate. Sledges, too, are only slightly modified versions of a sledge designed by the Norwegian biologist and polar explorer Fridtjof Nansen, over a hundred years ago. Made from laminated ash wood, they are lashed together by hand using leather thonging and string. This gives the sledge a great deal of flexibility when being hauled over rough and uneven surfaces.

It is said that in order to survive in a polar climate, a human needs to take in around 6,000 calories per day and this is reflected in the sledging rations which have been developed over the years. At Rothera a typical day's menu consisted of oatblock porridge made with full fat powdered milk, followed by tea, for breakfast; a bar of chocolate and a mug of hot sweet tea from a thermos flask for lunch (usually on the trail), then in the evening came the main meal of the day which was a choice of beef, mutton or curry stew made from reconstituted dried meat with butter added. Tea and buttered biscuits followed, and a mug of cocoa with a dash of rum and a few more buttered biscuits just before you crawled into your sleeping bag completed the daily menu. However, this diet was never sufficient to avoid weight loss and 'extras' were always added. With the addition of a few dried herbs and vegetables, some soup powder, a few tins of processed cheese, dried fruit and a jar of Marmite, even the most fastidious of palates could be satisfied.

I was introduced to the dog team which I was taking over from Rick Atkinson, who had been driving it for the last two years and has since settled in Alaska, where he trains and races dog teams. The teams had names and the team I was going to be responsible for was called the 'Picts'. The others were the 'Huns', 'Admirals', 'Players' and 'Gaels'. Each team was made up of between seven and nine dogs and was normally run on a 'centre trace', system, where one long line is attached to the sledge and the dogs are attached in pairs along the line, with a leader dog at the front.

My first run out with the Picts started off brilliantly, each dog pulling well and the leader, Lomond, complying with every command. All went well until we had run about half a mile, when suddenly the whole team stopped and turned to look at me, as if to say, 'Who the hell are you? You're not the normal bloke.' From then on it was an uphill struggle, but once mastered, driving a well disciplined team is one of the most satisfying activities I have ever undertaken and well worth the initial frustrations.

Shortly after Christmas the sea-ice broke up and autumn storms blew it out to sea. It made me feel trapped, confined to land, with only one direction to travel — up the ice ramp on to the island. It would be a few months before the sea-ice would form again, but it allowed access to Rothera by ship and soon the RRS *Bransfield* would arrive to resupply the base, transfer personnel and then depart, leaving just twelve men to winter-over.

The Wandering albatross (*Diomedea exulans*). With a wingspan of almost three metres it is the largest flying seabird. It follows the ship for mile after mile in seemingly effortless flight, only occasionally flapping its wings.

The further south we travelled, the calmer the seas became and some of the local wildlife came out to greet us. Here Adélie penguins swim alongside the ship 'porpoising' alternately under and over the water, taking a quick breath when in the air. In this picture strong back-lighting illuminates the splashes, producing an unusual photograph.

Opposite: Icebergs in evening light.

The American research vessel *Hero*, a small wooden boat with bows made from greenheart oak to give it the ability to push its way through pack-ice.

Opposite: Approaching the pack-ice of the Gerlache Strait, the mountains of the Antarctic peninsula can be seen in the distance.

Open pack-ice and icebergs form a typical Antarctic
seascape which is littered with wildlife. Crabeater and
Leopard seals relax on the ice floes along with Brown
Skuas and Dominican gulls.

Opposite: A Leopard seal (*Hydrurga leptonyx*) relaxing
on an ice floe, after finishing a meal of penguin. A
Brown Skua gull waits around for leftovers.

Ramming into heavy pack-ice in the Neumayer Channel. If you don't succeed on the first ram, you go astern and have another go.

Opposite: Evening sun and heavy pack-ice.

Top: A ski-equipped de Havilland Twin Otter aircraft, the workhorse of Antarctic air operations. It can land and take off in a very short distance.

Above: A view from the air of last winter's sea-ice breaking up as the summer advances. The ice will be about a metre thick and some of the larger sections will be about a kilometre across.

Opposite: The Royal Research Ship *John Biscoe* in Dorian Bay; Mount Français stands in the background on Anvers Island. This is as far south as the ship will go this early in the season, and from here we will be ferried south by Twin Otter aircraft.

Rothera Base from Reptile Ridge. Even in November solid sea-ice covers Laubeuf Fjord across to Pourquoi Pas Island, which is about twenty kilometres distant. In Antarctica the air is so free from everyday pollution that visibility is virtually unrestricted and on a good day it is often possible to see Alexander Island some 300 kilometres away.

Opposite: Approaching Adelaide Island from the north in 'dingle' flying weather.

Storm clouds brewing over Mount Mangin on Adelaide
Island. The blizzard that ensued imprisoned us in our
tent for the next seven days.

Opposite: The midnight sun. This photogaph was taken
at midnight during an ascent of Léonie Island. It
becomes almost a force of will to get the camera out
when your fingers feel like lumps of wood, but the
results are nearly always worth the effort and
discomfort.

Overleaf: In March the Royal Research Ship *Bransfield*
arrives at Rothera Base and must complete the resupply
before the sea freezes, closing the sea route for the
winter.

During a blizzard of this ferocity we listened to the BBC
World Service and played endless games of cards. As a
relief to the boredom we could go outside and take
photographs!

CHAPTER FOUR
WINTER

'Down in the deadly stillness, cut off from the world –
alone
Held in the grasp of the Ice King, on the steps of his
crystal throne:
Waiting returning sunshine, waiting the help we'll bring –
Wearily watching the hours go by, till the ship comes with
the spring.'

J. D. Morrison, 1903

'Irrrrrrrah! . . . Irrrrrrrrah! . . . Lomond you bastard!' Lomond, my leader dog, sensing the seriousness of my commands, pricked up his half chewed ears and for the first time in months, began to work to my every command.

We were descending the Shambles Glacier on Adelaide Island, after paying a visit to the old abandoned station on the south-west side of the island, some 70 km from Rothera. Visibility was poor, with much surface drifting snow. I was in the lead driving the Picts, followed by Vic August with the Admirals, then John Jewell and John Brindle with the Players bringing up the rear. In the bad conditions, I had taken a course slightly too far right, and had missed the 'safe' central corridor by about one hundred metres or so, ending up in an area of yawning crevasses. Out to my left lay a route which ran between two huge open crevasses, leading back across to safe ground in the centre of the glacier. I gave Lomond the command to turn left and follow this narrow road out of danger. Unknowingly, the other two teams had followed my trail and looking back, all I could see were three men silhouetted against a backdrop of snow, their dogs obliterated from view by surface spindrift as they followed between the gaping holes.

I cursed myself for making the mistake and for putting not only myself, but the rest of the party into a dangerous situation. Once on safe ground, Vic quite understandably spoke his mind in no uncertain terms, but as he spoke, the cloud started to break up and McCallum Pass came into view, so we decided to try and make it into Rothera that evening.

At the bottom of the long steep slope which rose to the head of McCallum Pass, we stopped for a rest. We all knew it was going to be a long, hard haul to the top but at least the snow surface was hard packed, which would help. Lomond, as usual, was sitting facing the rest of the team, waiting for the command to start. I shouted, 'Are you ready dogs? OK!' and the team was off at the gallop, then slowing to a trot and finally settling into the usual steady jogging pace, until the angle of the slope steepened and they ground to a halt. After a short rest, I set the team off again. They hauled for about thirty metres, then stopped and so it went on. Bit by bit, the three teams were coaxed and cajoled all the way to the top of the pass.

Overleaf: Storms in late summer can be quite spectacular. Strong winds blow spindrift from the top of icebergs that float around the bay and run aground just off the point.

From the top of McCallum Pass it is an eighteen kilometre run on level ground back to Rothera. The Picts, realising that they were returning to base, really pulled the stops out and we covered the distance in one afternoon, a distance which had taken three days to sledge on the outward journey, due to deep, soft snow conditions.

At the top of the Rothera ice ramp, all three teams stopped in order to put chain and rope brakes on the sledge runners before starting the descent into base. Vic led off first with a shout of 'Yippee!' followed by the Picts, then the Players. Showers of ice chippings flew into the air as the chain brakes dug into the iron hard surface, but even with all the brakes on, the sledges almost beat the dog teams to the bottom. As usual, most of the lads from base came out to welcome the returning teams, and to assist with putting the dogs back on the spans.

It had been nearly two months since the ship left, and the sea around Rothera was still just a mass of loose pack and brash-ice. It wasn't until early June that the freeze-up came, opening up sea-ice travel to the surrounding islands. At first, we made timid walks on skis out on to the ice and to local islets, but as the ice thickened our confidence grew, and before long plans were being made for sledge journeys across the ice to the mainland.

Before the sea-ice formed, the only direction we were able to travel was inland on to the island, but now all directions were open. After a while one becomes very complacent, tending to forget that what you are travelling on is only a very thin skin of brittle ice, covering water which is many fathoms deep!

June 22 was Midwinter's Day and a sort of Christmas atmosphere took over. The cook prepared a huge Midwinter dinner fit for a king and everyone took a couple of days off to celebrate. From then on it was all downhill to the return of the sun and the start of another Antarctic summer season. Once all the hangovers had subsided, everyone got down to work preparing equipment for the summer field operations. In the garage, our mechanic began the laborious task of stripping down all the ski-doos and rebuilding them, adding his own 'modifications' to the original design. In the sledge repair workshop, sledges, tents and camping equipment were prepared, just as last year's wintering party had done for us.

For me, the Antarctic winter was a period of inner discovery. Without the distraction of television, newspapers and the local pub, I managed to read all the books I had always promised myself I would read, but at home had never quite got round to reading. I also taught myself to play the flute to what I regarded as a fairly acceptable standard. Unfortunately no-one else appreciated my efforts so I was relegated to the boiler room for my practice sessions!

At midwinter the sun never rose above the horizon, even at midday, and the only indication that the sun existed at all was the eerie glow on the horizon which appeared at local noon, giving a wonderful golden tint to the surrounding white landscape. Through this period of twenty-four hour darkness, it was necessary to maintain a strict daily routine, as it was very easy to lose track of time and let yourself drop out of sychronisation with the rest of the base personnel. The midday glow told you that it must be lunchtime, but the rest of the day was total darkness which meant you had to eat and sleep by the clock.

The RRS *Bransfield* pays a last visit to Rothera, bringing with it a fresh supply of seal meat for dog feed. The seals are mostly Crabeaters and a few Weddell seals which breed in vast numbers around the Antarctic peninsula.

Within a few weeks of the sea-ice forming, sledge journeys were made to Blaiklock and Horseshoe islands by sledging the 'inside' route through the long, narrow fjords to the north and east of Pourquoi Pas Island. It was via this route that Nigel Young and I planned to travel to the old base on Stonnington Island in August. We left base with two dog teams and after being held up by bad weather for a couple of days on Pinêro Island, we made camp on the south side of Blaiklock Island, about forty-eight kilometres from Rothera. Further bad weather with temperatures down to −40°C put a stop to travelling for the next few days. On one of these 'lie-up' days, Nigel decided to harness up the Huns and run them on to the sea-ice for a bit of exercise. All went well, until the team reached the tide crack and the leading dogs stopped to jump it. All nine dogs bunched up and a full-blown dog fight ensued, with teeth, claws and fur flying in all directions. Both Nigel and I waded in trying to separate the snarling mass without being bitten ourselves and before they could do serious damage to each other. After 'picketing-out' the team, we found that one of the dogs, Tyke, had several deep bite wounds, and on closer inspection found that his backside had been severely ripped, so much so that his intestine was protruding from the wound. Our tent was cleared out and poor old Tyke carried in out of the wind. We gave the dog a sedative injection and a series of local anaesthetic jabs around the main wound, then spent the next hour stitching everything back together again. Nigel erected our small 'pup' tent nearby, into which we placed the by now well-drugged Tyke. After giving him a final dose of penicillin, we reorganised our tent and had a brew of tea.

The bad weather continued for the rest of the day, with strong gusting winds and heavy snowfall. That evening there was a hell of a disturbance outside, the dogs were barking and I could hear footsteps around the tent. I opened the tent door and peered out into the darkness, to be met by a large snow-covered black and white face out of which shot a long wet tongue which started to lick my face. Startled, I fell back into the tent, followed by a snow-covered Tyke. Pots and primus stove were knocked over and everything got showered in snow when the wayward hound decided to shake himself! Tyke had come round from his drugged sleep and, finding himself trapped inside the small pup tent, had clawed his way out through the side of the tent almost totally destroying it. We built a small wall of food boxes near to the tent to act as a windbreak, then tied Tyke to the leeward side where he remained for the rest of the night, slowly chewing out his stitches.

The following day we decided to make a run for Blaiklock hut, sledging back through the narrows between Pourquoi Pas Island and Blaiklock Island. By midday the weather had started to improve and the sun poked through the cloud, producing a beautiful solar parhelia which I thought must be captured on film. Letting go of the sledge, I pulled out my small pocket camera and jogged along beside the sledge until the team were just in the right position for the photograph. I snapped the picture and started to run after the dogs which were by now a long way ahead. I gasped as I stumbled and ran, trying to catch the runaway hounds, who having realised that they had lost their driver had broken into a gallop! I finally caught up with them after about a quarter of a mile and jumped on to the sledge brake while giving the command 'Aaaaah — Now' for the dogs to stop. After the team had stopped, they all sat down and turned to look at me as I hung on to the handlebars, gasping and coughing, as if to say 'We'll get you next time!'

Once at Blaiklock hut, another session of dog repairs got under way to replace the stitches that Tyke had chewed out the night before. By evening it was blowing a howling blizzard which kept us holed up at Blaiklock for several more days, but at least it was comfortable, and Tyke's injuries began to heal.

On the day we eventually said goodbye to Blaiklock hut, the sun was shining and it was calm. It was a great day to be alive, with good fast sledging on smooth sea ice with a hard surface all the way to the western end of Bigourdan Fjord. Here we stopped for our midday rest and a hot drink from a Thermos flask. Looking out across Laubeuf Fjord towards Adelaide Island, I noticed that the coastline was masked from view by a localised windstorm of some considerable ferocity, although where we stood there wasn't a breath of wind. I took a compass bearing on Rothera Point, and with a command of 'Are you ready dogs — ok', set out across Laubeuf Fjord. The further out into the fjord we sledged the windier it became, until we were engulfed in a strong northerly blow. We decided to push on, travelling on the compass bearing that I took earlier and still hoping to make it to base before nightfall.

By late afternoon, conditions deteriorated even further into white-out with driving snow, which forced us to stop and make camp. The wind was of such ferocity that it was only just possible to pitch the tent. Both dog teams were then fed but left in harness just in case we needed to make a quick getaway should the sea ice begin to break up. Throughout the night we remained fully clothed and took turns to sleep for an hour at a time. At 4.30 a.m. I took a look out of the tent door and there in the distance I could just make out the broad vertical beam of light made by the cloud searchlight which is located on the rocky point near to Rothera. This light was used by our base commander/meteorologist Kenn Back to measure cloud altitude, but tonight Kenn had very thoughtfully turned on the light to aid our return. I quickly took a compass bearing on the light, then woke Nigel. Missing breakfast, we packed the sledges and set off into the biting wind and early morning gloom towards the light. We sledged across the tide crack and on to Rothera Point at around 6.30 a.m., to be met by Kenn Back and Mike Sharp, who had waited up most of the night for our return. As it turned out, we had been forced to camp only half a mile from base and I often wonder what would have happened if, rather than stopping, we had given the dogs their head and made a run for base, trusting the instinctive sense of direction that Husky dogs seem to possess.

By now, with regular runs, the dog teams were in supreme condition. They all had clean, shiny coats and looked very healthy indeed. When on base, the dogs were fed on seal meat at the rate of around 2 kg of meat every other day. This called for regular seal hunting trips to be made in order to keep a good supply of meat for the dogs.

At first, the thought of killing a seal appalled me, not to mention the gutting and chopping that followed. I can still remember my first sealing foray out on to the sea ice and seeing the first animal shot and gutted — the memory will stay with me forever. After a while, I seemed to grow hardened to the whole thing and accepted it as a fact of life, for the dogs needed food. I didn't regard the seals shot as living creatures, but more as large lumps of dog meat. The purpose of sealing trips was in fact twofold: first and foremost to provide meat for the dog teams, but secondly to provide a fresh meat supplement to our own diet, as we ate most of the offal. Seal liver paté and stuffed seal hearts became regular favourites.

Towards the end of winter, I made a ski-doo journey with our mechanic Alan Tickle out from Rothera to the Dion Islands, to take a look at the Emperor penguins which colonised the islands. Emperors are the largest species of penguin living in Antarctica, standing almost one metre high and weighing in at between twenty and forty-six kilograms. They have a breeding cycle which is precisely timed so that their chicks, from eggs laid in May, reach independence by December or January, just as the sea ice begins to break up and food becomes plentiful.

Our intention after visiting the Dion Islands was to travel to the old Adelaide station, and from there overland back to Rothera. As we approached Avian Island, which is only a few hundred metres offshore from Adelaide station, we were confronted with rotting sea ice and a wide stretch of open water between Avian Island and the coast. We parked our ski-doos on the east side of Avian Island and walked over to the north side to visit our neighbours Sally and Jerôme Poncet. Sally and Jerôme had sailed their yacht *Damien II* down to the Antarctic peninsula the year before, with the intention of spending the winter in Marguerite Bay. *Damien II* was equipped with a retractable keel which enabled Jerôme to haul the boat out of the sea on to land as a base for the winter. Jerôme was a Frenchman and a very experienced sailor; his wife Sally was Tasmanian and a true adventurer. *Damien II* was a beautiful boat, made of steel and specially designed by Jerôme for cruising in Antarctic waters. Through the winter Sally and Jerôme made several long manhauling journeys, visiting Rothera and also the Argentinian station of San Martin, which is situated on the Debenham Islands about 100 kilometres away!

A few weeks later the aircraft returned to Rothera, marking the end to our winter of isolation. New faces and letters from home were very welcome, after almost seven months of detachment from the outside world. Soon the *John Biscoe* would arrive at Damoy Point air facility and summer field operations would begin.

The Costa del Ice!

Opposite: Jenny Island in Northern Marguerite Bay. Icebergs such as the one in the foreground are sculpted by the sun and waves, and can roam around the fjords for several summers before breaking up.

Overleaf: An iceberg trapped in winter sea-ice. The ski-doo at its base gives an indication of size.

My final summer in Antarctica was spent working with a geologist, Tim Jefferson, in the south east Alexander Island area, which meant working from Fossil Bluff field station some 400 kilometres south of Rothera. For two months Tim and I explored south east Alexander Island, travelling by ski-doo like an Antarctic chapter of Hell's Angels. We collected rock samples from remote, isolated nunataks, and on top of Coal nunatak discovered the remains of an entire fossil forest with superb fossilised tree stumps and ferns, dating back over 100 million years. At the end of the season we sledged back to Fossil Bluff via the Uranus glacier to await the aircraft which would then ferry us back to Rothera. For the best part of two weeks we waited, but the weather would not allow the aircraft to reach us and it was getting close to the time when the aircraft had to leave Antarctica for the winter. When the aircraft finally did arrive, I was on the point of preparing an inventory of supplies to calculate the possibility of spending the winter at Fossil Bluff!

At Rothera, the RRS *Bransfield* had arrived and the base relief was in full swing. All base personnel were working round the clock unloading stores and equipment from the ship, which was tied up by the ice-edge at Honeybucket Island while it pumped diesel fuel into inflatable rubber tanks sited on the hill above the base buildings.

Before long the resupply was complete, and it was time to say goodbye to Rothera. I walked down to the dog spans and, brushing away a tear or two, I said farewell to my team, the Picts, one by one: Lomond, the leader; Lil, who was one of two bitches in the team — the other one Vicky had sadly died during the winter; the two brothers, Malky and Fergy; father and son, Argus and Boot; and finally the back pair, Helix and Briggs, who formed the engine room of the team and were always hard workers.

From Rothera we sailed north to South Georgia to pay a short visit, then on to Port Stanley, Rio de Janeiro and finally Southampton, England — journey's end.

Icicles hanging from an iceberg drip with water in the afternoon sun. By using a fast shutter speed I have managed to 'refreeze' the droplets as they fall.

Opposite: Climbing the beautifully wind sculpted tail drifts on the southern side of Reptile Ridge. To be able to explore freely in such a stunning landscape is pure joy.

Gutting a Weddell seal to be used as dog feed. The meat
was also used to supplement our own diet as we
developed quite a taste for seal liver stew.

Opposite: New arrivals. A continuous breeding
programme is needed to keep the dog teams up to
strength. The endless comical antics of young husky
pups brought much enjoyment to the base personnel.

The Rothera dog spans, much slower than a ski-doo as a form of transport, but more environmentally friendly! The dogs lived outside all year round.

Opposite: The author with the 'Picts' below an unnamed peak at the northern end of the Wormald ice piedmont, during an early training journey lasting ten days on which we carried out an energy balance study of the standard sledging rations used at that time. In polar regions it is thought that you need to take in around 6,000 calories per day to remain healthy, but our diet only provided 3,800 calories and consequently we lost weight.

Hard going in deep 'softers' on the Fuchs ice piedmont.
At times like this, tempers fray as both humans and
dogs tire and the lead dogs become bored with no
landmarks to head for. What we now need is a good
strong blow to pack the snow surface down hard.

Opposite: The 'Admirals' coming into camp. Deep soft
snow conditions such as this can slow the daily mileage
down dramatically and on this day we only managed
three miles!

After being fed, the dogs settle down for the night. It is now that their wolf-like instinct takes over and with snouts pointing to the sky they give out an eerie howl in unison. They then sit and listen for a short while before repeating the chorus, and when no reply is heard they go to sleep. However, if another dog team is nearby, a continuous exchange of howls could go on all night.

Opposite: Beautiful layered cloud over Lewis peaks to the north of Rothera. The sun will soon disappear behind them for the winter.

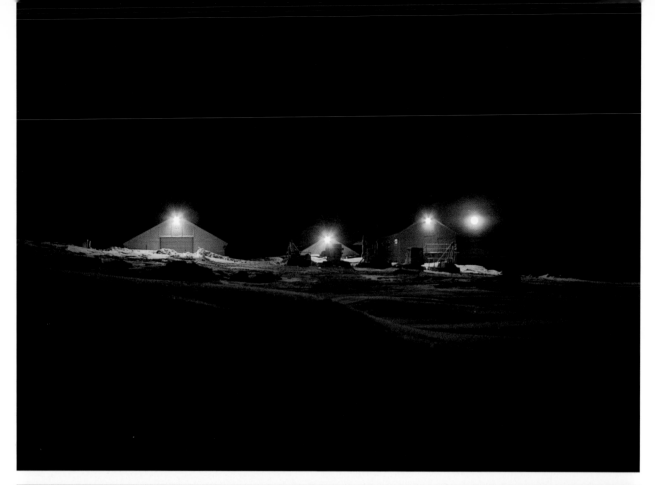

Above: Rothera Base at midday, close to midwinter.

Top: Midwinter. The light from the base illuminates the surrounding snow. On the right is the moon which circles the sky twenty-four hours a day. A sturdy tripod and film of reasonably fast speed is required for this type of winter shot.

Opposite: Diesel exhaust from the generator shed is condensing in an air temperature of −35°C at midday. The Lewis peaks are silhouetted to the north by the midday sun glow.

Looking north during winter the sky is alive with light, but the sun fails to rise.

Opposite: Cutting up frozen seal carcasses for dog feed is a regular chore throughout the winter. The carcasses are frozen so hard that a chainsaw and felling axe are needed to do the job.

In the evenings it was time to catch up on world news by listening to the BBC World Service on a small, short wave radio. There are no newspapers or televisions in Antarctica and I didn't miss them!

Opposite: The sun returns producing 'Earth shadow'. It brought back a sense of warmth to the frigid winter landscape and was a tonic to those on the base who suffered from the depression of 'winteritis'.

Above: A natural archway in a stranded iceberg near Blaiklock island. You could walk all the way through the berg.

Opposite: A beautiful solar parhelia over Ryder Bay, with Rothera Base in the foreground towards the end of winter.

Overleaf: Making a run for home after a night camped out on the sea-ice in a strong blow. A small break in the weather gave us the chance we needed to run the last half mile to safety.

Above: Unloading mobile huts onto the ice-foot at Rothera to be used as shelters at the air strip some distance from the base.

Top: Fossil Bluff field station at 71°21'S, 68°17'W. Built on the east coast of Alexander Island on 20 February 1961, it has been occupied intermittently ever since, including ten winter occupations. This was the jumping off point for Tim Jefferson and I for our fieldwork on south-east Alexander Island.

Opposite Top: The RRS *Bransfield* returns to Rothera to resupply the station and transfer personnel.

Opposite Bottom: The yacht *Damien II* hauled out on the beach at Avian Island to serve as a base for its owners Sally and Jerôme Poncet. Jerôme specially designed the boat for cruising in Antarctic waters, with a steel hull and retractable keel. The keel, apart from enabling the boat to be hauled on to a beach, was hollow and held five tonnes of diesel fuel to power the yacht's inboard engine when pushing through pack-ice.

Fossil ferns and tree stumps found on Alexander Island
date back over 100 million years. These particular fossils
were found on Triton nunatak and are proof that
Antarctica must have been a very warm place at one
time.

Opposite: Tim collecting rock samples from Triton
nunatak on south-east Alexander Island. Large melt-
water pools can be seen on the surface of the King
George VI ice-shelf, even at 72° South!

Emperor penguins *(Aptenodytes forsteri)* near to the Dion
Islands, Marguerite Bay. Emperors are the largest living
species of penguin, at almost one metre in height and
between twenty and forty-six kilograms in weight.

CHAPTER FIVE

THE FUTURE

'I am hopeful that Antarctica in its symbolic robe of white will shine forth as a continent of peace, as nations working together there in the cause of science set an example of international co-operation.'

Admiral R. E. Byrd, U.S. Navy

This was the dream of Admiral Byrd, and in 1961, only four years after his death, the dream came true. An international treaty was signed by all the nations who, in that year, had an interest in Antarctica, and wished for peaceful co-operation and international goodwill to prevail for at least the next thirty years. The basic provisions of the Antarctic Treaty were as follows:

1. Antarctica is to be used for peaceful purposes only. Military personnel may be employed there but only on scientific, essentially peaceful work.

2. The freedom of scientific investigation and co-operation which characterised the International Geophysical Year (1957-58) is to continue.

3. All scientific observations are to be made freely available to all, and scientific personnel are to be exchanged.

4. All political claims (in particular claims to territory) are to be frozen for the thirty year duration of the Treaty.

5. Nuclear explosions and the dumping of radioactive waste are banned.

6. All stations and equipment are open to the inspection of observers appointed by the nations concerned.

And so, in 1961 Antarctica became a 'continent of science', and the provisions of the Treaty became a reality. To date there are more than fifty research stations maintained in Antarctica, all working together for the benefit of mankind, proving that science has no political or national boundaries. The Antarctic Treaty was a remarkable milestone on the road towards conservation and preservation of the Antarctic environment, but it was very much a temporary solution and will be reviewed in 1991 should any of the signatory nations require change. What about the long term future, post-Treaty?

The future is, to say the least, uncertain, which places Antarctica at a fork in the road. One direction leads to the continuation of peaceful co-operation and goodwill, generated by the framework of the 1961 Treaty and ultimately, through increasing international support, to full protection under the heading of 'world park' for ever. To take the other fork in the road would be unthinkable, leading to large scale commercial exploitation and despoliation of the last pure wilderness on this planet.

The fact is that no-one actually owns Antarctica, and there is nothing to stop anyone from going there to begin uncontrolled prospecting for minerals. Once commercial exploitation begins, any official control will be very difficult to implement, and by that time the damage will be done. As we have seen very recently, even with the best will in the world, accidents will always happen. Consider the environmental damage caused to the Alaskan coastline when the oil tanker *Exxon Valdez* ran aground on Bligh Reef, spilling 10.5 million gallons of oil. A 650 kilometre oil slick polluted beaches along the Alaskan coastline and devastated wildlife, leaving 37,000 sea birds dead. The Exxon Oil company were only able to recover one per cent of the spill. This cannot be allowed to happen in Antarctica.

If no formal controls are agreed very soon, then scientists may find themselves sharing Antarctica with the 'sledge hammer to crack a nut' mentality of oil men and mineral miners. They would have to endure the painful sight of the fragile ecosystems which they have travelled to Antarctica to study being destroyed.

Should anyone think that commercialism is not a threat to the future of Antarctica, just think of the environmental destruction of the past. The whaling and sealing industries of the eighteenth and nineteenth centuries bear full witness to the thoughtless annihilation of Antarctic wildlife with only profit in mind. Abandoned shore-based whaling stations litter the coasts of South Georgia and many other Antarctic islands as a sad reminder of the mass slaughter which reduced southern whale stocks to only a fraction of those thought to have existed before whaling began.

Antarctica is still relatively free from the pollution that the rest of the world has had to suffer. It is a stunning, pure and pristine wilderness which for the moment only tolerates the presence of scientific bases, which by their mere existence produce polluting waste and, in some cases, even this is unacceptable. If small, uncommercial scientific bases do not afford Antarctica the respect it deserves then what hope is there if full scale mining operations begin? Unfortunately, there is strengthening speculation in the existence of precious mineral and oil deposits, which makes Antarctica an irresistible target for a resource-hungry world. It would take only a small increase in world mineral prices to make the mining of Antarctic minerals a financially attractive proposition. The environmental disruption of such commercial operations due to the increase in shipping, air traffic and human population, not to mention the physical damage to the landscape caused by mining itself, is unthinkable and totally unacceptable.

The discovery of the Antarctic ozone hole caused by the use of chlorofluorocarbons as aerosol propellants, and the slow global warming due to the 'Greenhouse Gases' produced by deforestation and the burning of fossil fuels, has illustrated in a dramatic way just what damage we are doing to our planet's ecosystems. This has brought world opinion firmly round on the side of conservation.

Environmental organisations such as Greenpeace are now playing a vital role in Antarctica by carrying out valuable research and monitoring the activities of other nations who maintain stations there. Greenpeace also maintains a base on Ross Island, only a stone's throw away from Antarctica's best known landmark, Captain Scott's hut. By maintaining a base in Antarctica, Greenpeace will have greater influence among the other Treaty nations when it comes to posing the idea of Antarctica becoming a world park.

Opposite: The unique Antarctic wildlife, such as the Crabeater seal, is well adapted to the polar environment, but extremely vulnerable and sensitive to disturbance and environmental change. The disruption caused by clumsy commercialism would destroy their finely balanced lifestyle forever.

It cannot be stressed enough just how important the Polar regions are to world climate, and in turn to the future existence of mankind on this planet. Antarctica contains almost ninety per cent of the world's fresh water, and if this were to melt completely it would raise sea levels by over fifty metres world wide. This would put many of the world's major cities under water and some entire countries would be eliminated altogether. It is my hope that common sense will prevail, and that the world's governments will take notice of world opinion which points strongly to the protection of Antarctica as a world park for all time, remaining within the present framework of the 1961 Treaty.

Mankind should invest in Antarctica as a place which future generations can enjoy, just as I did, and hope to do again in the not too distant future. Its fate is in our hands. The despoliation of the landscape that commercial mining would engender, or an oil spill on the scale of the *Exxon Valdez* disaster, would be catastrophic to the fragile balance of nature which is so important to us all. The only real solution must be total international protection as a world park.

It will be man's last chance to protect for future generations the last great, unpolluted wilderness on Earth from his own headlong slide towards global environmental catastrophe.

The culling of Reindeer on South Georgia is necessary to
keep the size of the herds down to the number of
animals the surrounding grazing can readily support.

Opposite: Faraday Base on the Argentine Islands is a
typical example of human occupation on the coastline of
Antarctica. Peaceful scientific research carried out from
installations such as this is compatible with the
Antarctic environment.

Damien II and *Champi* are just two of the increasing
number of private yachts which visit Antarctic waters
each year. This type of adventurous sailing is dangerous
and some people might ask 'Who is responsible for
these vessels should they find themselves in difficulty?'
However, as a fellow adventurer, I can fully understand
the sense of freedom that the crews seek and therefore
would never discourage it.

Opposite: The tourist ship *Lindblad Explorer* on the west
coast of the Antarctic peninsula. If controlled in a
positive way, tourism promises to be an important
Antarctic industry, providing the means for ordinary
people to enjoy the Earth's finest treasure.

BIBLIOGRAPHY

Anderson, W. Ellery, *Expedition South*, Travel Book Club, London, 1957.

Cameron, Ian, *Antarctica: The Last Continent*, Cassell & Company, London, 1974.

Fuchs, Sir Vivian, *Of Ice and Men*, Anthony Nelson, 1982.

Judd, Alfred, *The Conquest of the Poles*, T. C. & E. C. Jack Ltd, Edinburgh.

King, H. G. R., *The Antarctic*, Blandford Press, London, 1969.

Mountevans, Admiral Lord, *The Desolate Antarctic*, The Travel Book Club, London, 1949.

Ommanney, F. D., *South Latitude*, Longmans, Green & Co, London, 1938.

Ralling, Christopher, *Shackleton*, BBC Publications, 1983.

Rymill, John, *Southern Lights*, The Travel Book Club, London, 1939.

Shackleton, Sir Ernest, C.V.O., *South*, William Heinemann Ltd, London, 1925.

Shackleton, Sir Ernest, C.V.O., *Shackleton in the Antarctic*, William Heinemann Ltd, London, 1909.

Stonehouse, Bernard, *Animals of the Antarctic*, Peter Lowe, 1972.

Strange, Ian, *The Bird Man*, Gordon & Cremonsi, 1976.

Woods, Robin W., *The Birds of the Falkland Islands*, Anthony Nelson, 1975.